Harmony In Marriage

More Than Sex

Catherine Roberson MA, JD

*Priority*ONE
publications
Detroit, Michigan USA

Harmony in Marriage: More Than Sex
Copyright © 2012 Catherine Roberson

All scripture quotations, unless otherwise indicated, are taken from the HOLY BIBLE, NEW INTERNATIONAL VERSION®. ®. Copyright ©1973, 1978, 1984 by International Bible Society. Used by permission of Zondervan. All rights reserved.

Scripture quotations marked (AMP) are taken from the Amplified Bible, Copyright © 1954, 1958, 1962, 1964, 1965, 1987 by The Lockman Foundation. Used by permission.

Out of reverence and honor for God's Word, the word Bible is capitalized throughout this work.

All rights reserved. No part of this publication may be reproduced, stored in a retrieval system, or transmitted in any form or by any means – electronic, mechanical, photocopy, recording, or any other – except for brief quotations in printed reviews, without the prior permission of the publisher.

*Priority*ONE Publications
(800) 596-4490 Nationwide Toll Free
URL: http://www.p1pubs.com
E-mail: info@p1pubs.com

ISBN 10:   1-933972-29-7
ISBN 13: 978-1-933972-29-9

Cover design by Crump Industrial Design, LLC
Interior design by Christina Dixon
Editing by Patricia Hicks

Printed in the United States of America

Endorsements

Harmony in Marriage: More Than Sex by Catherine Roberson is a well thought out and biblically based book on the marriage relationship, which would benefit any couple to read. Whether married or contemplating marriage, this book is a powerful and insightful resource to have. The book is complete with biblical references, theoretical principles and experiential examples on the marriage relationship. Those persons engaged in marriage counseling could benefit greatly by having couples read this book and then engage in the counseling session. It can also be used as required reading in a Pastoral Care and Counseling course in school. I recommend the book without reservations.

James T. Roberson, Jr., PhD
Dean, Shaw University Divinity School
Raleigh, North Carolina

Harmony in Marriage: More Than Sex touches on all areas of marriage where conflict can arise. Each chapter gives practical application on how to apply the principles of God and have a marriage that is filled with peace, harmony and is God edifying.

Pastor Willie Richardson
Senior Pastor, Christian Stronghold Church
Philadelphia, Pennsylvania

Dedication

Writing this book has truly been a labor of love. It required much time in prayer and meditation, as well as, many hours of reflection, research, and scripting the message. However, I could not have done this without the love and support of my family.

First, I dedicate this book to my husband, Pastor David L. Roberson, the love of my life and my spouse of more than thirty years. Without him there would be no story for me to tell about marriage. Also, without him I would not have had the passion to write this book. He was also a contributing writer for Chapter 8 entitled, "Managing Your Finances."

Second, I dedicate this book to my parents, Arthur and Thelma Cartwright. Although they have both gone to be with the Lord, they will always be with me in spirit and in my heart. I thank God for both of them because they were dedicated and loving parents who raised me with Christian values.

Third, I dedicate this book to my children, Crystal Wilson and Justice Roberson. I thank them for being my gifts from God when I prayed to have a family. Without them, I would not know what it means to be a mother and to raise a Christian family. Also, I would like this book to be a legacy to pass on to them and their children.

Table of Contents

Dedication 5

Preface 9

Foreword 11

Introduction 13

1. Self – Identity 17
2. Leaving and Cleaving 27
3. Mutual Support and Respect 35
4. Submission 45
5. More Than Sex 51
6. Intimacy – Two Becoming One 59
7. Communication Is Basic 69
8. Managing Your Finances 81
9. Appendix A – Mutual Support: Survey Results 97
10. Appendix B – Managing Finances: Survey Results .. 103
11. Appendix C – Sample Budget Format 108
12. Author Bio 109

Preface

It is truly amazing how the many varied instruments in a symphony orchestra can come together in perfect oneness, or sweet harmony. This is only possible when the will of each player yields to the will of the conductor. Marriage is much like a symphony orchestra. Each spouse brings varied gifts and talents that play out in a marriage. If they come together as one, they can make beautiful music together. If they bring their former single-minded attitudes into the marriage, then the result can only be a cacophony of disharmony. This dissonance, if allowed to continue unchecked, will result in a rapid descent into the downward spiral of discontent in every area of the marriage. The highest percentages of cases that we see in our lay-Christian counseling center are marriages that have reached this point. Sometimes couples need a guide or conductor to help them understand and see how they can find their way back up and out of the cacophony. What we find in most cases, is either the absence of a conductor, or a failure to yield their wills to the will of the right conductor—God the Holy Spirit.

Catherine Roberson, author of *Harmony in Marriage: More Than Sex*, brings a diverse background of education, training, and experience to bear on this topic. She is an attorney, an active minister of the gospel, a pastor's wife of thirty-plus years, and the mother of two adult children who themselves are also ministers of the gospel. I have known her for twenty-years and have watched her grow as a godly wife and mother, a professional, a spirit-filled minister of prayer, a mentor, and a dear friend. Therefore, I can truly attest to the wisdom evident in the pages to follow. She has captured the essence of what it takes to have a successful Christian marriage. I encourage you to continue reading and to keep an open mind and heart as you seek to develop the sweet sound that comes from *Harmony in Marriage: More Than Sex*.

Rev. Valerie Crump, Associate Minister
*Director - Biblical Counseling Ministry and
Christian Research & Development (CRD) Training Extension
New Hope Missionary Baptist Church, Southfield, MI*

Foreword

Among the multitude of marriage resources that are helping couples at every stage of their relationship maintain their commitment to marriage; a new text takes it place. *Harmony in Marriage: More Than Sex* joins the line of marriage books such as, "Love and Respect," "Before You Say I Do," and " Can Two Walk Together" that will be relevant for years to come.

This easy to comprehend book filled with stories, illustrations and points of life application demonstrates to couples the truth of the Word relating to being single and becoming one flesh. *Harmony in Marriage: More Than Sex* is a refreshing look at marriage from the eyes of a woman who has learned to love the blessings of submission, respect and honor. Rev. Catherine Roberson has over thirty years of marriage from which she draws insight and wisdom for the next generation. She has many practical lessons to teach those who desire to model maturity and spiritual growth.

My husband often reminds me what the preacher said as we stood at the altar taking our vows, His words were, "Look at her closely, she will be constantly changing from this day forth." Rev. Roberson is aware of the continuous changing dynamics between couples as they evolve in their relationship to Christ and their intimacy with one another. Her research-based and experiential text address the issues such as finances, respect and poor communication, that usually get in the way of a satisfying fulfilling sexual experience between husband and wife.

Whether you are newlywed, approaching the seven year itch or an empty-nester this book will help you experience the harmony in marriage that God has destined for you to achieve.

Rev. Dr. Sabrina D. Black
Author, Counselor, Life Coach, International Speaker
Founder - Global Projects for Hope, Help and Healing
President - National Biblical Counseling Association

Introduction

"LOVE AT FIRST SIGHT"

One Friday evening in September, 1978, a young woman named Catherine called a friend and asked if he knew of a "party going on" that weekend. After all, the weekend had just begun and after working all week, Catherine was looking to socialize with some other young adults.

"Sure," he answered. "It just so happens that my wife and I are having a barbeque this evening. We have invited some other persons over to watch the fight tonight. How about coming over and joining us?" Larry said.

"Will there be any other single persons there, or is this going to be an old married couple's thing?" Catherine asked.

"Yes, we have invited quite a few single persons, and I'm sure you may even know some of them. A couple of them went to college with you, so I'm sure you will enjoy yourself," Larry answered.

"Great. I'll see you later," Catherine said with a smile. She could hardly wait to go out and have a good time that night.

Later that evening, Catherine arrived at the home of her friends and she greeted everyone with a warm smile. "The barbeque smells delicious," she said.

The hostess replied, "We are glad you came and dinner will be ready real soon. Would you like to join everyone in the backyard? We have set up the T.V. outside so we can watch the heavy weight championship fight between Muhammad Ali and Leon Spinks."

After entering the backyard, Catherine began speaking with a few persons she knew and she enjoyed listening to the "cool" music playing on the stereo. The social atmosphere was enhanced with music by Marvin Gaye and other entertainers, such as Earth, Wind and Fire. It was a perfect autumn evening with all of the right persons networking with one another.

All of the guests were casually dressed in blue jeans and sweaters and were enjoying the music. Most of them had just gotten off from work and they were enjoying the company of the other guests. Catherine was glad to see several classmates from college and she was feeling quite self-confident while socializing with everyone.

Just as she was surveying the crowd checking out who was there, in walked an attractive young man she had not met before. "My goodness, he is quite handsome and he has a great smile," Catherine thought to herself. Then she heard her friend Larry say, "Hey Mighty, I'm glad to see you. Come on in and I'll introduce you to some of my friends."

Catherine turned her back and started talking to one of her friends. After all, she didn't want to be caught staring at this young man who she thought was so tall, dark and handsome. She could feel her blood warming up inside of her and rushing through her body.

A few minutes later, her friend Larry came over to Catherine and said "By the way, David, this is Catherine. I don't think I've introduced you to her." At that moment, Catherine turned around and saw David's bright brown eyes and the biggest smile she had ever seen. He said to her, "Nice to meet you. How are you?" "I'm fine," she replied. They talked for a short time then she excused herself and went into the house.

When she returned to a different area in the backyard, she noticed him staring at her from a distance. He came over again and said to her, "The fight is about to start. Who do you think is going to win?" "I don't know," Catherine said, "but I'm hoping Muhammad Ali wins because I think he's cute." Then she blushed because she saw the sparkle in David's big brown eyes again.

They watched the fight together, while laughing and enjoying the warm night air. The evening seemed to pass by very quickly as they shared a feeling of mutual admiration for each other. At the end of the party, David asked Catherine if he could see her again in the near future.

It has been more than thirty years since David and Catherine met, and they still enjoy each others love and companionship. Surely, there must be truth to that old cliché, "Love at first sight."

Harmony in a relationship is a quality that benefits all persons involved. Both married and single persons will find this book to be very helpful in several ways. The targeted audience of this book includes two distinct groups of persons.

First, the primary audience is married couples: both newly wed and mature couples. One recurring message in the book is that marriage is a relationship that requires continuous adjustments that must be made by both husband and wife. It is a mutual commitment between two spouses that requires work every day.

Second, singles thinking about getting married will also find the information in this book to be very helpful. It will give them an inside perspective regarding what to expect after they become married. Also, it will be a valuable resource to correct some myths single people may have about marriage.

Developing "harmony in marriage" is similar to creating harmony with music. Just as it takes many hours of practice and rehearsals to help separate musical instruments in an orchestra to blend their melodious sounds together, husbands and wives must commit much time and effort to develop harmony in their relationship. Married couples must learn to communicate and work together to strengthen their relationship. Hopefully, their efforts will result in building a loving marriage lasting a lifetime.

Chapter 1

Self-Identity

"For I know the thoughts that I think toward you, says the Lord, thoughts of peace and not of evil, to give you a future and a hope. Then you will call upon Me and go and pray to Me, and I will listen to you."

Jeremiah 29:11-12 NKJV

One of the oldest questions asked by ancient philosophers has been, "What is my purpose in life?" The Greek philosophers Plato and Socrates spoke about this topic many centuries ago. This is a very fundamental question we ask ourselves even today. As Christians, we believe that each of us, men and women, were created by God in his image;

however, we commonly ask ourselves, "What is my purpose for living?"

Many adults live all of their lives seeking their purpose and self - identity. Some of us just live our lives, day by day, without any set goals or objectives. Others graduate from college and pursue careers which turn out to be unfulfilling. Others may find a comfortable job or position in life, just settle for joining the proverbial "rat race," and accept a decent paycheck in place of being truly fulfilled by what they do.

Traditional marriages require two persons, male and female, to make a commitment to each other and to God. Hopefully, the loving relationship between husband and wife is composed of two whole persons who bring an understanding of who they are into the partnership. This understanding is based on their self - identity. However, maintaining balance in the marriage relationship is an art and a challenge.

Self-identity takes time and maturity to understand. Often, it even changes after one thinks he or she has established their identity. The change may occur to either one or to both spouses as he or she adjusts to their new roles in their marriage. These roles include becoming committed to each other as husband and wife and perhaps later becoming parents.

Recently, I read an interview in the August 25, 2010 issue of *People Magazine* entitled "My Own Story" written by Sandra Sobiera Westfall. It was about a well - known woman who was the mother of two young children, and she had just gone through a divorce. Her former husband was a famous athlete who was known around the world. She described what seemed to be a very secure and wealthy life - style that she enjoyed during the six years of marriage. She had been very happy with their marriage relationship, and she loved their two young children, ages 3 years and 9 months old, very much. Her famous husband was one of the wealthiest men in the world.

One day, she was visited by a journalist from a national television network. He asked her if she would consent to an interview. She was quite flattered, so she said "Yes." However, she was shocked when he asked her if the rumors of infidelity about her husband were true. She was not aware of any of the facts the reporter asked her to comment about.

Nine months after this interview, she was divorced from her billionaire husband. When asked how she felt, she responded that she was relieved. She said that although she loved becoming a mother, the celebrity schedule of her husband was very demanding, and she never really adjusted to all of the traveling and time he spent away. As a matter of fact, during the six years of their marriage they spent most of their time apart even when she had two pregnancies and gave birth to two children. However, she lived the life of modern day royalty and had an abundance of everything.

She said the divorce happened so quickly, she did not have time to really feel bad about it. On the contrary, she actually felt quite relieved because now she was free to live her life just as she wished. Before her marriage, she lived with her parents. So this would be the very first time she would truly be living "on her own," and she could explore who she really was.

Who was this young woman? Her name is Elin Woods, former wife of Tiger Woods. Although she had been married to one of the most well known and wealthy men in the world, she was still attempting to find out her "self-identity."

A fundamental part of being a complete person is having the freedom to be you. Spouses should respect each other's freedom. The book, *Boundaries in Marriage*, describes the importance of freedom in a marriage. The author states that freedom is a prerequisite of love. If someone controls us, love is not possible. Control results in slavery, not love. The ability for each partner to allow the other to be a free, separate person is one of the hallmarks of a solid relationship.[1]

A good marriage among two complete people is one in which they keep their individuality and space, and this actually serves to strengthen their relationship. After they have been apart, they share each partner's experience.[2] The author also explains that a problem marriage is one in which one partner sees time apart, separateness and space as a threat. This spouse may feel that separateness means a lack of love or abandonment.[3]

I found it to be very interesting that the author points out there is not a certain "amount" of separateness that is good or bad for all couples. However, the amount has to be negotiated with wisdom so that the "we" does not suffer. There is no absolute, but couples who have a fundamental orientation toward freedom – the ones who do not see separateness as a threat are able to work out the details.[4]

We must keep in mind how your freedom is affecting your spouse. There is a warning for this type of situation in

---

[1] Cloud & Townsend, 101
[2] Cloud & Townsend, 102
[3] Cloud & Townsend, 103
[4] Cloud & Townsend, 104

the Bible in Luke 10:27 where it states, "Love your neighbor as yourself." In other words, don't do anything away from your spouse that you wouldn't want them to do while you are away. Perhaps Tiger Woods should have learned this value before he went golfing around the world and left his wife at home.

My Own Story

When I first met my husband, I was a young woman with a career. I was employed with the State of Michigan as a community development manager. I had completed a B.A. Degree from the University of Michigan and a Juris Doctorate Degree from Rutgers Law School. I enjoyed meeting new persons and working with local city officials to develop new businesses and urban development projects.

I was also very active in supporting political candidates seeking public office. It was during my volunteer work with a candidate running for Governor of the State of Michigan that I met David my husband. I was 28 years old, and I considered myself to be very independent, both financially and emotionally. Having grown up during the 70's, I saw myself as being a "liberated young woman" with many options in life.

During the first year of marriage, we both had careers. My husband was employed as a financial manager at a well known automotive corporation. He was well liked by his employer, and he had a very positive future.

However, after our second year of marriage, he announced to me that he had decided to become a minister. I was completely taken by surprise. Although he was very devoted in attending church each week and even taught a Sunday School class, I never thought he would become a minister. My first concern was, "What does that make me? Does this mean that I must be a minister's wife?"

Also, I wondered if that meant we would not be able to go out and socialize with our friends as we had in the past. I did not know any other women who were married to ministers, and I had no idea of how a minister's wife was supposed to act. I was a modern, educated, liberated woman who did not want to be restricted in the way I enjoyed living my life. During that year, I had just given birth to a beautiful little girl and was still adjusting to being a new mother. It was just too much changing in a short period of time. "Whatever happened to the career woman identity I had developed for myself?"

I was even beginning to feel angry, and I asked, "Why would my husband make this decision without talking to me about it. After all, his decision to become a minister would change our entire lifestyle and even have a definite influence on our daughter and other future children we may have."

After discussing my feelings with my husband, he kindly told me that he had no choice. He said he felt that the call to become a minister was very strong, and it was coming from God. He assured me that he loved me, and he cherished our marriage, but he could not ignore this special calling in his life. I was still upset, and I called a dear aunt and asked her to take a trip with me to Nassau. I explained that I needed to get away and spend time with her to get her advice. I respected her as a mature wife and mother, and we had a very close relationship. She accepted my invitation, and during our three day trip, she listened to my concerns. Afterwards, she told me to pray about it and let the Lord speak to me. That was the best advice anyone ever gave me.

After I returned home, I prayed for about two weeks alone each night. After putting my baby daughter to bed, I asked the Lord to guide me so I would not make a rash or emotional decision. Finally, one night He answered. I remember reflecting on how I was raised as a child. Even though I had been raised by a loving mother, she had been divorced since I was very young. Also, even though I had a very good relationship with my father, I missed not having two parents who lived together at home. As a young child growing up, I would often pray at night that my parents would make up and get back together, and that we could live as one happy family. But that never happened. I wondered why other children had parents that seemed to be content with each other, but mine were not. I felt a deep emptiness in my heart, as a child and as a young adult that no one could seem to fill.

Finally, I realized that I never wanted to feel that way again. Nor did I ever want my baby daughter to experience that feeling of loss and sadness. Also, I knew in my heart that my husband loved me and was sincere about his calling to become a minister. So I realized that I had to give up a great part of my selfish desires and make a commitment to support my husband and the unity of our family. This was the price I was willing to pay to have a stable home and family. I was spiritually led to trust God with our future.

Today, after more than 30 years of marriage as a minister's wife, and having raised two young adults who have both graduated from college and have good careers, I know now that I made the right decision.

Chapter 1 – Self-Identity
Review Questions

1. What is a fundamental question men and women ask themselves?
   _____
   _____
   _____

2. What is a loving marriage relationship comprised of?
   _____
   _____
   _____

3. Does someone's self-identity develop quickly? Does it change?
   _____
   _____
   _____

4. What is a fundamental part of being a complete person?
   _____
   _____
   _____

5. What is a prerequisite of love between husband and wife?
   _____
   _____
   _____

6. What is a signal of a problem marriage?
   _____
   _____
   _____

7. Is there a certain amount of separateness that is good or bad?
   _____
   _____
   _____

8. How is the amount of separateness negotiated?
   _____
   _____
   _____

9. Does our freedom affect our spouse?
   _____
   _____
   _____

10. What Scripture in the Bible tells us how to treat others?
    _____
    _____
    _____

Chapter 2
"Leaving and Cleaving"

"For this reason a man will leave his father and mother and be united to his wife, and they will become one flesh."
Genesis 2:24

The first few years of marriage are a big adjustment for everyone. It's not easy changing from being a single person to being married. As a single adult, you are just responsible for yourself and fulfilling your needs and desires. These may include social, physical, intellectual, and emotional requirements. However, after becoming married, your perspective changes. Now you have another person, your spouse that you must be considerate of. Just like you have needs, they too have needs which must be met.

It has been stated in the commentary of the *Life Application Bible*,[5] that God gave marriage as a gift to Adam and Eve. They were created perfect for each other. Marriage was not just for convenience. It was instituted by God, and the man leaves his parents and, in a public act, promises himself to his wife.

After marriage, the roles of the family members change for not just the husband and wife, but also the parents. Likewise, there are other outside influences which must be dealt with, such as friends and siblings. This can be explained by giving a few examples.

Family Birthdays

Cheryl and Josh have been invited to a birthday dinner for Cheryl's dad. Cheryl and Josh have been married for one year, and her family has always celebrated the birthdays of both parents and her siblings by having a celebration. The date of the dinner is on an evening when a good friend of Josh is having a bachelor's party before his wedding.

Cheryl asks Josh to attend her father's dinner party with her instead of going to the bachelor party. Josh says that he would prefer to go his friend's party. Cheryl is upset because she knows that her father will be very disappointed if she and Josh don't attend. Since Josh is concerned about being a good husband, he calls his uncle Eric, who is a minister, for advice.

First, Eric asks Josh, "Do you love your wife?" Josh responds, "Of course I do. She means the world to me, and

---

[5] *Holy Bible, New International Version (NIV) Life Application Study Bible* (1995). Wheaton, Illinois, Tyndale House Publishers, p. 10, note: Genesis 2:24

she is a very good wife." Eric continues by reminding Josh that as her husband, he must put her well being and happiness before his friends. He reminds Josh of the Scripture in 1 Peter 3:7-8 which says:

"Husbands, in the same way be considerate as you live with your wives, and treat them with respect as the weaker partner and as heirs with you of the gracious gift of life.... Finally, all of you, live in harmony with one another; be sympathetic, love as brothers, be compassionate and humble."

Eric advises Josh that he must learn to place the needs and desires of his wife before those of his friends. His commitment to his wife must take priority over that to his friends and family members. Eric shares with Josh that after 25 years of marriage, he still must prioritize his time to accommodate the reasonable requests of his wife. Josh agrees that because he loves his wife, he will attend her father's birthday dinner with her.

Relationships with Friends Often Change

Friendships of the newlywed couple often change. The husband and wife have made relationships with others years before they were married. Similar to parents, the role of friends also needs to change. Instead of sharing their most confidential feelings with friends, husbands and wives must become each other's most close confidants.

Steve and Kate were both very sociable and had many friends before they were married. Steve's male buddies had always gone out together and hung out at the local clubs. Shortly after Steve married Kate, his best buddy Jeff asked him to go to the club with him. Steve told Jeff that since he was married, he had decided not to hang out with him like before. However, if Jeff wanted to go to dinner with him and Kate, that would be fine.

Kate also had several close friends. Chris was one of them, and they had attended the same college. During those years in school, they shared their deepest secrets with each other, including the men they dated. Later, they were also bridesmaids in each other's wedding.

After Chris got married, she continued to confide in Kate about the problems she had in her marriage. Although Kate felt somewhat uncomfortable, she listened to all the problems Chris shared with her. Some of the information shared was quite confidential and intimate. Several years later, Kate got married. However, unlike Chris, Kate chose to respect the privacy of her marriage and did not share intimate details with Chris. As a result of this, their relationship was not as close as it was in the past.

My Own Story

When I first married my husband, David, he had many friends who are no longer in our life. He has always been a very sociable person, and he loved to play pinochle, a card game which he would play all night long. I had never played and did not understand the game, so he decided to quit playing cards and stay home with me rather than play cards with his friends.

Also, before he married me, he loved to go dancing at the Webb Wood Inn in Detroit, MI on Wednesday nights. This was a disco bar where singles met, danced, and enjoyed drinking. However, after we were married and he accepted his call to ministry, he no longer went. Now we teach Bible study class on Wednesday nights. He had to leave that lifestyle because he wanted to maintain our marriage.

I also gained a new mother-in-law, Mary, that I didn't know before we were married. Although she lived in Mississippi, my husband loved her very much and would call her at least once each week, just to talk. She was always very polite and kind to me whenever we spoke on the phone.

There were times when David would call and ask her for advice, and she was always willing to help him. However, early in our marriage, David called his mother because we had an argument. He wanted her to support his position and to correct me. I remember what she told him, and it has always stayed with me. Mary told my husband that she did not take sides when her grown children disagreed with their spouses. If asked, she would give her opinion based on her own experience of being a wife and mother, but it was left up to the couple to work out their own problems.

I respect my mother-in-law to this very day. She is very wise, and she never tried to interfere with my relationship with my husband. Even though my husband still calls her very frequently, she realizes that her son loves me as his wife, and he places me first in his life. She also respects our privacy and does not give her opinion about our marriage unless one of us asks her to do so. I've learned over the years that Mary supports our marriage and not just her son. There were times when she would remind David that he had a very good wife, and he should not be acting a certain way.

In conclusion, if your adult children are getting married, here are some things that will help your son or daughter cleave to their mate:

1. Do not offer unsolicited advice. If you are deeply concerned about something, pray and allow the Lord to guide you regarding when to give advice.

2. Accept the fact that your son or daughter is an adult, so do not attempt to dictate to them.

3. Realize your son or daughter's first allegiance is to their spouse, not you, and now their spouse comes first.

4. Do not take sides. Allow your adult children to develop their own way to resolve disputes.

5. When giving financial assistance to your son or daughter, don't give more money than you are willing to lose without a grudge.

Each of the examples given above show how relationships often change after a person gets married. What do these examples show us? First, they show that our relationship with our spouse must have priority above all other human relationships. Also, they show that marriage changes our relationships with our parents, family members, and friends.

Chapter 2 – Leaving and Cleaving
Review Questions

1. What does Genesis 2:24 say about changing relationships after a man and wife are married?

   _____
   _____
   _____

2. What is the first significant adjustment a person must make after becoming married?

   _____
   _____
   _____

3. What other relationships are changed after becoming married?

   _____
   _____
   _____

4. What does 1 Peter 3:7-8 say about how to treat your wife?

   _____
   _____
   _____

5. What priority do the needs of your spouse have in relation to all other persons and family members?

   _____
   _____
   _____

6. How important is maintaining privacy in your marriage?
   _____
   _____
   _____

7. Will your commitment to your spouse require you to change your prior lifestyle?
   _____
   _____
   _____

8. Regarding adult children, when should "in-laws" give advice?
   _____
   _____
   _____

9. Should a mother, father, or in-laws take sides in a marital dispute?
   _____
   _____
   _____

10. How can adult children and "in-laws" set limits on the amount of money they loan or give to family members?
    _____
    _____
    _____

Chapter 3
Mutual Support and Respect

"Submit to one another out of reverence for Christ."
Ephesians 5:21

As long as husbands and wives support each other daily, their actions will strengthen their respect for each other. However, when one spouse fails to support the other, it places an unbalanced weight on the relationship. Also, over time, if one partner fails to support his or her spouse on a regular basis, resentment may begin to develop. Eventually, the neglected spouse may begin to distance themselves from the other because they feel as though they have been "taken for granted" for too long. This leads to a downward spiral of marital discontent, and it may begin to accelerate over a period of time.

If you are interested in stopping this cycle, you may ask: "What can be done to remedy this situation?" First, one spouse must communicate his or her feelings to the other. Hopefully, the other spouse will listen attentively, and seriously take notice.

Second, the other spouse must be willing to change their behavior. Perhaps, they will have to make more of an effort to be more considerate of their spouse's needs. If these two things do not occur, the "downward spiral" of marital discontent will continue to grow. Eventually, this will lead to more serious problems in their marriage. It is my opinion that mutual support is another way to show mutual respect for each other.

For example, Joyce Meyer, a well-known celebrity, has built a career in ministry and television evangelism over the past 25 years. Also, she has authored many books about Christian faith and righteous living. I have noticed that Joyce Meyer commonly refers to her husband as being very supportive during her television programs and in her books. Often she has stated that her husband, David, is her biggest supporter and she credits him for being her partner in the success of her career.

Joyce has stated that David runs the business portion of her ministry. He is responsible for the staff and all the business contracts and related operations. Joyce openly admits that although her husband is not on camera and is not a public speaker, she could not do what she does without him. Joyce also has explained that David supports her emotionally. Often he comforts her and calms her down when she becomes frustrated or disappointed with the stresses of her career. She acknowledges him as being the person chosen by God to be her soul mate and lifetime partner.

Joyce admits that she did not always cooperate with her husband, and her poor attitude had a negative effect on her ministry. She shares a testimony in one of her books, and explains that one day she prayed to the Lord for her ministry to grow. The Lord spoke to her and said: "I really can't do anything else in your ministry until you do what I have told you to do about your husband. You are not showing him proper respect. You argue with him over minor details, things. You should let go and drop. You have a willful, stubborn, rebellious attitude. I have dealt with you about it over and over again, but you just refuse to listen."[6]

Even though Joyce Meyer gave an explanation of why she had to learn to cooperate and respect her husband, she learned that she would not be happy or successful unless she did so. She tried to justify her poor attitude by referring to being abused as a young child. However, eventually she realized that, in spite of this reason, she had to cooperate with her husband.

Husbands and wives should feel comfortable depending on each other. I believe that my spouse needs me to help him accomplish certain goals, and similarly, I need him to help me accomplish many of mine. One day after I had helped my husband finish a project, he said "You gave me the confidence to believe I could complete this assignment. Before you offered to help, I was about to just give up. I doubted that I would be able to do this. Now I see that I can do this with your support and assistance. You helped to restore my self-confidence; I love you honey."

---

[6] Meyer, 185

I was truly surprised when he said this. My response to him was, "Thank you dear. I was just doing what I thought a good wife should do. I saw you were experiencing a lot of stress due to the pressure of starting the new project, and I wanted to help. Now that we are working together, I see you smiling again. Just seeing you relaxed and smiling again makes me feel so much better."

Later, I reflected on another time when I had injured my foot, and it became progressively more painful. I had banged my foot on a piece of furniture, and it began to swell. After visiting the foot doctor, he told me I had an infection on my toe, and he cut a part of the toe nail off. Although I was able to walk, it was much more difficult to do house chores.

One evening, David saw that the dishes were stacked up in the kitchen sink. Instead of complaining, he washed all of the dishes, put them away, and swept the floor. While he was doing this, I purposefully went into the next room and watched television. After he finished, he came into the room and said "I just got tired of seeing those dirty dishes." I responded, "Thank you dear; I appreciate your help." We spent the rest of the evening relaxing and watching T.V.

The next day, David washed dishes again after I had finished cooking a full breakfast. Like before, he cleaned the kitchen. This time he did not make any remarks or comments. This is an example of how my husband shows support for me when I need help. It may sound small, but I greatly appreciated it. The fact that he did not make remarks when he completed the chores on the second day, made his help even more special.

My husband has also supported me in my career choices. After working many years in business development for the State of Michigan, I decided to begin a career in ministry. I believed the Lord had called me to work as a partner with my husband, who was serving as the Pastor of a church in Southfield, MI. I shared by calling to ministry with him and wanted to be prepared. I decided to enter seminary and obtain a Master's Degree in Pastoral Ministry.

David supported me during the entire three years while I was working full time and going to Graduate school. I was very grateful because I knew that many of his male associates in ministry, as well as some of the officers and members of our church, did not believe that women should be allowed to serve in the pulpit. However, in spite of the biased views of others, David supported my efforts, and after graduating from Marygrove University in Detroit, I was ordained at our church as a Baptist Reverend in 2005.

There are many authors who have written books about marriage based on the concept that respect is the most important thing a man desires from his wife; and similarly, wives greatly need love from their husband. I believe that both husband and wife crave mutual respect and support.

Dr. Emerson Eggerich wrote the book entitled, *Love and Respect*. He writes that based on research of many married couples, "respect" is the most important thing husbands crave in a marriage. Also, he states that "love" is the most important thing wives crave. He even gives examples of how he aggravates his wife "unintentionally" by leaving dirty clothes and towels lying around the house.[7] This aggravates his wife

---

[7] Eggerichs, 21-22

who is quite interested in keeping a neat house. I believe that if he knows his behavior aggravates his wife and he is not willing to change, then he is being "disrespectful" to his wife.

He may profess his love for his wife verbally, but if his actions do not demonstrate his love, then I believe his words are just empty gestures. Although he talks about the concept of "unconditional respect" and "unconditional love," I believe that actions speak louder than words. Having been happily married to the same man for more than 30 years, I believe that mutual support is the same as mutual respect. Also, I believe that both husbands and wives crave love and respect, and showing respect for his wife is an expression of love. Similarly, showing lack of respect is a sign of lack of love.

I believe a better model of what drives the relationship between husbands and wives is given in another book entitled, *How to Improve Your Marriage Without Talking about It*. It describes the difference in feelings possessed by males and females. The authors, Dr. Patricia Love and Dr. Steven Stosny, have written this book based on the premise that the behavior of females in a marriage is based on fear and the behavior of males is based on shame.

They explain that women are more loving, compassionate, and caring. However, it is riskier for men to express too much love and compassion because that will make them feel more like failures as lovers, providers, protectors, and parents. This is the feeling of shame that men are always attempting to avoid.[8]

This theory of "fear" possessed by women and the avoidance of feeling "shame" by men is the basis of many power struggles in marriages. Both Drs. Patricia Love and

---

[8] Love and Stosny, 21

Steven Stosny agree that although women's fear and men's shame are unconscious, these inner feelings affect their behavior in their marriage. For example, power struggles happen when two people fight to protect themselves from shame and fear. She wants him to do what she wants so she doesn't have to feel anxious, and he wants her to give in so he doesn't have to feel like a failure. They try to control each other or even force the other to submit. This power struggle results in more resentment and hostility which increases the fear and shame.[9]

This is a very interesting theory which is the basis of an entire book on maintaining a good relationship with your spouse. The authors have also conducted marriage conferences and workshops based on this behavioral theory about men and women. I believe that the concept of balance in a marriage is presented more clearly by Dr. Love and Dr. Stosny.

Men and women by their nature are made to think and act differently. Therefore, husbands and wives must take time to become more knowledgeable about their differences and respect each other accordingly.[10]

---

[9] **Love and Stosny**. 34
[10] **Mutual Support & Respect,** Survey Questions, Catherine Roberson, M.A., J.D., Appendix A

Chapter 3 – Mutual Support and Respect
Review Questions

1. What does Ephesians 5:21 say about submission for husbands and wives?
   _____
   _____
   _____

2. How do husbands and wives strengthen respect for each other?
   _____
   _____
   _____

3. What happens when one spouse fails to support their mate?
   _____
   _____
   _____

4. What two things can be done to stop the downward spiral of marital discontent?
   _____
   _____
   _____

5. What else does mutual support show to your spouse?
   _____
   _____
   _____

Mutual Support and Respect

6. List four ways you can show mutual support for your spouse.
   _____
   _____
   _____

7. What is a sign of showing a lack of respect?
   _____
   _____
   _____

8. What is the theory of Dr. Love and Dr. Stosny that is used to explain the difference of male and female behavior in marriage?
   _____
   _____
   _____

Chapter 4

Submission

"However, each one of you also must love his wife as he loves himself, and the wife must respect her husband."
Ephesians 5:33

Submitting to another person is often a misunderstood concept. It doesn't mean becoming a doormat. Christ submitted His will to the Father, and we honor Christ by following His example. When we submit to God, we become more willing to obey His command to submit to others. That means to subordinate our rights to theirs. In a marriage relationship, both husband and wife are called to submit.

For the wife, this means willingly following her husband's leadership in Christ. For the husband, it means putting aside his own interests in order to care for his wife. Submission is rarely a problem in homes where both partners have a strong relationship with Christ and where each is concerned about the happiness of the other.

The apostle Paul speaks to wives about submission in Ephesians 5:22-24 where he writes, "Wives, submit to your husbands as to the Lord. For the husband is the head of the wife as Christ is the head of the church, his body, of which he is the Savior." I interpret this as meaning that wives are to respect their husbands and demonstrate this respect by their actions. Perhaps, this will require her to be more considerate of her husband's needs and directions. Granted, changing ones behavior is not always easy. However, as Christians, we must rely on the Bible and pray to help us to manage any situation in life.

Similarly, Paul speaks to husbands about submission in Ephesians 5: 25 – 28 KJV, "Husbands, love your wives, just as Christ loved the church and gave himself up for her to make her holy, cleansing her by the washing with water through the word, and to present her to himself as a radiant church… In the same way, husbands ought to love their wives as their own bodies. He who loves his wife loves himself."

I interpret this as explaining to husbands how they should respect and love their wives just as Jesus loved the church and "gave himself up" for her. This means Jesus was willing to die or sacrifice himself for the church. In the same way, husbands should be willing to sacrifice their life to protect his wife. This includes giving up their selfish wants and desires and putting the needs of their wife before their own.

Paul goes further to explain to husbands they need to attempt to make their wives holy by "cleansing her by the washing with the water through the word." This means that husbands must be knowledgeable of the Word of God, the Scripture, so they can minister to their wives and lead by living a righteous life. By doing this, husbands will help their wives to grow spiritually. This is a responsibility expected of the husband which makes him worthy of respect and honor. This also means that men should take time to study the Scripture and actually get to know their wives: spiritually, psychologically, and physically. This requires husbands and wives to spend quality time together so they can get to know each other better. *(This topic will be discussed in more details in chapter 6)*

Married couples must apply the Word of God to their lives. As long as husbands and wives submit to each other daily, their actions will strengthen their respect for each other and their marriage. However, when one spouse fails to submit to the other, it places an unbalanced weight on the relationship. Over a period of time, resentment begins to develop. Eventually one spouse may begin to distance himself, or herself, from the other because they feel he or she has been taken for granted or disrespected for too long. This leads to the previously mentioned downward spiral of marital discontent, and it may accelerate over a period of time.

You may ask yourself, "What can be done to remedy this situation?" Well first, the offended spouse should communicate his or her feelings to the other. Hopefully, his mate will listen attentively and seriously take notice. Second, the other spouse must be willing to "change" his or her behavior. Just apologizing and saying I'm sorry is not enough.

Rather, the offender must demonstrate a change in their pattern of behavior over a period of time.

It truly takes two committed persons to make a marriage work. This requires both husband and wife to dedicate themselves to supporting each other. As long as married couples use Jesus Christ as a role model in submitting to one another, their marriage will become stronger. Jesus demonstrated submission in His life by:

- Submitting to His Father's will and not His own

- Demonstrating His love for the church by sacrificing His life
- Receiving love from the church in response to His sacred sacrifice

Similarly, the love between husbands and wives will grow as they demonstrate their love for one another by submitting their lives to each other. Jesus showed us by his example: there is no greater gift than to be willing to submit yourself to another.

I must testify that after more than 30 years of marriage, my husband and I have learned to put Christ "first" in our lives and live in loving harmony with each other. As a result, we have peace in our home and respect for one another. Yes, we have had some very challenging years along the way, but we have relied on our belief in Jesus and the Word of God as our anchor, and we have been able to endure and make it through.

Chapter 4 – Submission
Review Questions

1. What does Ephesians 5:33 say to husbands and wives?
   _____
   _____
   _____

2. What example should husbands and wives follow in submitting to one another?
   _____
   _____
   _____

3. What does submission mean to the wife?
   _____
   _____
   _____

4. What does submission mean to the husband?
   _____
   _____
   _____

5. What does Paul say to husbands about attempting to make their wives holy?
   _____
   _____
   _____

6. How do spouses strengthen their respect for each other?
   _____
   _____
   _____

7. What happens when one spouse fails to submit to the other?
   _____
   _____
   _____

8. How did Jesus demonstrate submission in His life?
   _____
   _____
   _____

9. What did Jesus show us by His example?
   _____
   _____
   _____

10. What benefits may couples receive by putting Christ "first" in their life?
    _____
    _____
    _____

Chapter 5

More Than Sex

"Behold, thou art fair, my love; behold, thou art fair; thou hast doves' eyes within thy locks: thy hair is as a flock of goats, that appear from mount Gilead."

Song of Solomon 4:1 KJV

Romance in a marriage is like fudge on an ice cream sundae. Just as fudge adds flavor and extra enjoyment to ice cream, romance adds more enjoyment to a marriage. Many couples remember the romantic times they spent together while dating and during their honeymoon. However, several years after being married, many couples get into a set routine or schedule and neglect spending romantic time together.

Romantic is a word used to describe a feeling. There are many other similar words which include: loving, amorous, passionate, fond, tender, sentimental, idealistic, and hopeful.[11] A romanticist is a person described as a dreamer, visionary, or idealist. [12]Romance in marriage includes all of these adjectives and feelings. A healthy marriage is composed of two persons in whom the couple shares their dreams, visions, and future desires with one another.

Romance in marriage is vividly described in Song of Songs written by King Solomon. This book of the Bible was written to tell the story of King Solomon and his bride; including their courtship, love and marriage.

In Song of Songs 4: 1-3 , Solomon romantically describes his bride:

> "How beautiful you are, my darling! Oh, how beautiful!
>
> Your eyes behind your veil are doves. Your hair is like a flock of goats descending from Mount Gilead."
>
> "Your teeth are like a flock of sheep just shorn, coming up from washing… Your lips are like a scarlet ribbon; your mouth is lovely."

Solomon goes on to describe the other parts of his bride's body. He ends by saying in Song of Songs 4:7 , "All beautiful you are, my darling; there is no flaw in you."

---

[11] Oxford American Large Print Thesaurus, p. 725, Oxford University, Inc. , New York , 2006
[12] Ibid

Similarly, the bride describes the love she feels for the king. Song of Songs 1:2-4 states:

> "Let him kiss me with the kisses of his mouth-
> for your love is more delightful than wine.
> Pleasing is the fragrance of your perfumes;
> your name is like perfume poured out.
> No wonder the maidens love you!
> Take me away with you – let us hurry!
> Let the king bring me into his chambers."

These words may seem strange to us, but their feelings of love and admiration are clearly understood. The lesson to learn from reading this is that communicating love and expressing admiration in both words and action to our spouse can definitely enhance every marriage. There is truly wisdom in the Word of God.

Ways to Renew the Romance in Your Marriage

I believe there are ways to renew the love shared between husband and wife. Here are a few suggestions that have worked in my marriage.

First, remember to express your love and appreciation for your spouse each day. This can be done by giving them a compliment on how nice they look or how thoughtful they are. You can show appreciation by smiling at them and sharing a nice conversation with them. You can also surprise them by picking up a gift for no particular reason, just to let them know you were thinking about them. Wives can make an effort to cook a favorite meal for their husband, or if the husband enjoys cooking, he can prepare a special meal for his wife.

Second, devote time to romancing your spouse. This can be done in a variety of ways, so be creative in coming up with different ideas. If you have young children, hire a baby-sitter and plan an evening with another couple to have fun. This will help you remember the fun you had with your spouse when you were dating. If possible, plan a weekend away, for just the two of you or with another couple. This will greatly help to refresh your love life together. If you can't afford to go away for the weekend, perhaps you can ask a grandmother or aunt to have the kids come to their house and spend the night. This will allow you and your spouse to go home and share dinner alone and relax together. You may even pick up a carry out dinner and go home and watch a movie and even take a bubble bath together. This is a time to be creative and to allow your romantic impulses to be freely expressed. You may be surprised by all of the "old romantic things" you will remember from the "good old days."

Third, start planning a project together. I have found that relationships are strengthened when partners work together to accomplish a common goal. In this case, I mean working together on a pleasant and enjoyable project. This doesn't include paying the bills, raking leaves, or cleaning the dog's area which may be filled with "dog poop." I'm talking about planning a project you "both" will enjoy. For some couples that project may be learning to play golf together, or perhaps planning a vacation.

My husband and I enjoy playing golf together during the spring and summer months in Michigan. We look forward to spending "uninterrupted" time together on the golf course. This allows us time alone to escape from our other responsibilities of pastoring a church or being mentors, parents, and grandparents.

We also enjoy planning long vacations together. After completing several seven to ten day cruises and making several trips to Mexico, we started traveling around the world together. Our first twelve day international trip was a Mediterranean Cruise. We traveled to four countries: Greece, Turkey, Egypt and Jerusalem. We started planning the trip about ten months before our departure in May, 2010. We had completed a budget, saved our money, and we had time to look forward to traveling. Several months before the trip, we spent time reading about the different "ports of call" and cities where we planned to visit. About a month before leaving, we began shopping together for the trip.

Looking back on everything, we both enjoyed the trip very much, and we took a lot of photos and made a DVD from the pictures. I wrote a journal during our twelve day Mediterranean Cruise, and reading it today brings back many beautiful memories and experiences. We both considered this to be a once in a lifetime experience that we shared, and it brought us much closer together.

Now we are planning our next international trip in July, 2012 to the Holyland, Israel, and Jordan for thirteen days. We are really looking forward to enjoying this next "once in a lifetime" adventure together. I intend to write another journal about this trip as well, and one day have all of my travel journals published. These will be precious memories which we can share with our children, and grandchildren, and other family members.

I encourage married couples to continue to develop their relationship and be creative in renewing their romance. All experiences of marital bonding do not take place in the bedroom. Be adventurous and make your dreams come true. One of the most rewarding feelings of intimacy with your spouse is sharing together a dream you have both worked on to come true.

If you would like to view a DVD which tells a story of a couple developing a loving marriage relationship, I recommend seeing "The Story of Us." The actors in the movie are Bruce Willis and Michelle Pfeiffer.

Chapter 5 – More Than Sex
Review Questions

1. What does the word romantic describe?
   _____
   _____
   _____

2. What is a healthy marriage?
   _____
   _____
   _____

3. Which book of the Bible describes romance in marriage?
   _____
   _____
   _____

4. What lesson can we learn from reading romantic Scripture?
   _____
   _____
   _____

5. What are three ways to renew the love between husband and wife?
   _____
   _____
   _____

6. What is one of the most rewarding feelings of intimacy with your spouse?

_____
_____
_____

Chapter 6
Intimacy ~ Two Becoming One

> *"My lover is mine and I am his; he browses among the lilies.*
> *Until the day breaks and the shadows flee, turn, my lover,*
> *and be like a gazelle or like a young stag on the rugged hills."*
> Song of Solomon 2:16-17

Intimacy is a basic part of a marriage relationship. It's a way for the two spouses to become bonded as one. Although God created man and woman to come together and multiply by having children, sex often changes after the first few years of marriage. Research has shown that love and sex may have two different meanings to men as compared to women. Males and females may have different feelings about their sexual relationship with their spouse.

"Intimacy" is a word commonly used to describe human relationships. It is defined in the Oxford American Writer's Thesaurus as a noun meaning: closeness, togetherness, affinity, rapport, attachment, familiarity, friendliness, friendship, amity, affection, warmth, or confidence.[13] Although many people associate the word "intimate" with sexual relationships, I believe it can relate to different types of relationships. The key factor in an intimate relationship between two persons is that they "know" each other's behavior and habits, as well as their likes and dislikes. Some examples of intimate relationships include: brothers and sisters, parents and children, husbands and wives and close friends. Knowing someone takes time, and people must share experiences with one another before they develop an intimate relationship.

For example, there was a time when I had to take physical therapy treatments for a problem I had with my back. During the treatment, the therapist stated that I should continue an exercise routine after therapy classes ended. She suggested that I visit an exercise facility located near my home and perhaps ask someone to attend exercise classes with me. This would be a way of having a support plan to help encourage me to continue to be active and maintain muscle strength. Although I thought about asking my husband to accompany me to see the new exercise facility, I knew that in the past we had done so, and he was never interested in taking exercise classes. Therefore, I decided to ask my sister-in-law to go with me because I knew she was looking for a

---

[13] *Oxford American Large Print Thesaurus* (2006) NY, NY Oxford University, Inc.

place to exercise, particularly during the fall and winter. This decision was based on the intimate relationship I had with my husband and my knowledge that he would not like to join a health club.

The *International Encyclopedia of Marriage and Family, 2003*, states:

> "Conceptions of intimacy usually address one or more of three phenomena: intimate interactions, intimate relationships, or intimate experiences. Intimate interactions are communicative exchanges between people.... Intimate relationships, in contrast, imply a series of interactions between two individuals known to each other. Intimate experiences are the feelings and thoughts people have during, and as a result of, their intimate interactions. Intimate relationships are those in which partners know each other well and who maintain positive, loving feelings towards the partner who they know so well."

Research has documented that most men are greatly influenced by the physical elements of an intimate relationship, while women are more influenced, over time, by the emotional elements of intimacy.[14] My observation over the years is that the first and "overly romantic" phase of an intimate relationship begins with the initial attraction between a man and a woman. It continues during dating for several months or even several years. During this time of "courting,"

---

[14] Cutrer and Glahn, 383

each party sees the best aspects of their lover's personality and often they feel a sense of euphoria. The feeling of love is strong and the physical attraction is often uncontrolled.

The second phase of the relationship develops when each party has made a definite commitment to date each other exclusively. This may continue through a period of time while continuing to date exclusively and later after, a formal engagement has been announced. The feeling of love is still very exciting, and each person may day-dream about their lover. Anticipation grows as each person makes plans to get married and become husband and wife.

The third phase is during the first year of marriage. This is still the "honeymoon" stage when spouses are infatuated with their mate, and love-making may be a daily activity. It's like letting a young person loose in a candy store which is filled with all of the different candies he can imagine. Although God created man and woman to come together and multiply by having children, sex often changes after the first few years of marriage.

Getting to know your spouse takes time, and that's a good reason to wait awhile before starting a family. First, it's important to get to know the personality of your spouse and see him or her in different moods. Second, it's nice to have your spouse all to yourself before having a child. It's common knowledge that having children changes the relationship between husbands and wives because it requires both spouses to make additional adjustments.

You may ask, "How does having a child relate to intimacy between a husband and wife?" Well, before the baby arrives, all of your love and affection was focused on your spouse. However, after the baby arrives, fathers must learn to share the love they once exclusively received from their wife with the new baby. This means that mom may not always be "ready" or "in the mood" for making love after caring for the baby and working all day, either inside or outside of the home. This will be a big adjustment for everyone. Learning to be a good parent takes time, effort, and energy. Therefore, the focus of your relationship will shift from being "passionate love mates" to becoming responsible parents.

More mature spouses, married more than ten years, may also experience adjustments to their sexual intimacy. I have observed that as couples age, their bodies change due to physical changes and sometimes illness. Although a couple's love-making may "slow down," it does not mean they cannot continue to express love and consideration to one another. If the adjustment is too difficult for them to manage, I recommend they seek out the advice of a physician or sex therapist. I have also been informed that some married couples have improved their love making abilities by taking hormones under the supervision of a physician or licensed health professional.

Differences Between Husband and Wife Regarding Sex

William Cutrer and Sandra Gavin wrote in *Sexual Intimacy in Marriage*, a description of several ways men and women approach sex differently. When I read the book, there were four observations that are very interesting.

First, the authors discussed "timing." They stated that while women proceed more slowly in moving from sexual excitement to reaching an orgasm, men respond quickly in a physical manner. Dr. Cutrer referred to other persons saying,

"Men are like light bulbs, women are like electric irons" or "men are like gas stoves, women are like crockpots." Dr. Cutrer also observed that "men and women differ significantly in the time needed between foreplay and orgasm." While the majority of women surveyed needed at least fifteen minutes of stimulation following arousal to reach orgasm, the average man was able to go from sexual excitement to orgasm in three to five minutes.

Secondly, Dr. Cutrer wrote about the different sexual needs of men and women. He stated that for men, sex is necessary to fulfill primarily strong physical needs; while for women, sex is needed primarily for emotional needs, with physical needs which may accompany them. My response to this observation is that perhaps this explains why women seem to enjoy cuddling and being held by their husband after love-making.

Third, Dr. Cutrer explained how the feelings of men may affect their love making and is different from how feelings affect women. For example, he stated that if a man and a woman have an argument, some men can stop in the midst of an argument, have sex, and return to the fight. However, most women would have a very difficult time having sex while still being angry or upset with their mate.

Fourth, Dr. Cutrer describes how differently men and women respond to being enticed before having sex. For women, the environment and surroundings are more provocative to get her in the mood; whereas, men are not necessarily affected by the environment. Men can be enticed or aroused to make love just by the sight of an attractive woman whether or not she is clothed.

Dr. Cutrer gives many more examples of the differences between men and women in approaching sex. For more details, I recommend reading the book which is very interesting and will stimulate much discussion between husbands and wives. It may also be helpful for spouses who wish to improve their sexual relationship.

In conclusion, the way men and women express their love through sexual intimacy for one another may vary. However, I believe it is the responsibility of both the husband and the wife to communicate their feelings of love and appreciation to their spouse daily. As I discussed earlier in this chapter, "intimacy" in a marriage includes more than having sexual relations with your spouse.

Chapter 6 – Intimacy - Two Becoming One
Review Questions

1. What word is commonly used to describe human relationships?
   _____
   _____
   _____

2. What is the key factor in an intimate relationship between two persons?
   _____
   _____
   _____

3. What has research documented regarding how men and women differ in what influences an intimate relationship in marriage?
   _____
   _____
   _____

4. What are the three phases of an intimate relationship between men and women leading up to marriage and in the first year of marriage?
   _____
   _____
   _____

5. How is living with someone while married different from dating someone?
   _____
   _____
   _____

6. Why is it a good reason to wait a while after getting married before starting a family?
   _____
   _____
   _____

7. What adjustments do mature couples married more than ten years experience?
   _____
   _____
   _____

8. What are four examples of how men and women differ in their sexual relationship with their spouse, as described by Dr. William Cutrer and Sandra Gavin?
   _____
   _____
   _____

9. What is the responsibility of both spouses to do daily?
   _____
   _____
   _____

10. What is the basic lesson you learned about intimacy in marriage?
   _____
   _____
   _____

Chapter 7
Communication is Basic

"Let no corrupt communication proceed out of your mouth, but that which is good to the use of edifying, that it may minister grace unto the hearers."
                                                    Ephesians 4:29 KJV

Communication between husband and wife is essential to maintaining harmony in a marriage. Many people underestimate the importance of effective communication. I believe that communication between spouses is as basic as oatmeal served for breakfast. You may ask: "What does oatmeal have in common with communication?" Everyone has heard about the importance of eating breakfast each day. Oatmeal is a very basic type of breakfast that offers many benefits. As a child, my mother served me oatmeal or some form of hot cereal every morning before going to school.

First, oatmeal is nutritious and provides fiber and energy for your body. Second, oatmeal can be served plain, or it can be spiced up with cinnamon, raisins, and syrup. Either way, it is still quite healthy for your body. Third, after eating a bowl of oatmeal, my stomach felt full, and I was able to concentrate on my work all morning at school.

Similarly, communication with your spouse is very basic. Effective communication connects or assists you in connecting with your mate. It is like the fiber oatmeal provides for your body. Without fiber, you body will soon feel empty and will lack energy. Likewise, without communication, your relationship with your mate will become weaker and soon loose its strength. Just like your body needs to be fed nutritious food, your marriage relationship must be maintained by communicating effectively with your spouse.

Also, like oatmeal, communication between spouses can be done using different techniques. It does not have to be done in the same manner. A variety of forms of communication may be used to share your thoughts and feelings with each other.

Finally, after communicating with your spouse openly and effectively, both persons should feel satisfied, just as the oatmeal satisfies your stomach. Good communication is important to eliminate distractions in building a sound relationship. Also, it will allow you to concentrate on working together in solving the larger challenges in your life.

Merriam-Webster Dictionary defines the word "communicate" as meaning: "to engage in an exchange of information or ideas." It lists the following words as being related: "correspond, converse, talk, message, bond, commune, relate."

How Can I Communicate Effectively To My Spouse?

Most commonly, persons think they communicate by talking to their spouse. Although this is one way to communicate, there are many other ways that may be effective. Here are seven different ways to communicate with your spouse.

1. Communication by Body Language

Have you ever spoken with someone, and they did not look at you directly in your eyes? I have, and the first message I received was lack of sincerity or trust. It is very important to make eye contact with your spouse when speaking with them.

I remember as a child, my mother would often speak to me about doing my chores. If I knew what she was about to talk to me about, I would look down or act like I was busy doing something else. She would soon lose her patience and say in a loud voice "Cathy, look at me when I'm speaking to you." This meant that she had picked up from my body language that I didn't want to listen to her.

Similarly, when your spouse speaks with you about something that may be of concern to them, you should stop what you are doing and look at them. Eye contact is important to let your spouse know you are listening to them. Also, it let's them know you are concerned about what they have to so. The lack of eye contact may send a negative message to them.

2. Communication by Our Service

There is an old cliché: "Actions speak louder than words." In other words, in addition to telling your spouse you love them, you should show them by your actions. For example, both my husband and I worked during the time we had children and raised our family. There were many days when I came home from work, picked up our kids from school, cooked dinner, washed dishes, did homework with our two children, and put them to bed.

Does this sound familiar to some of you? By the end of the day, I would often be so tired; I would not feel like speaking to my husband or being bothered to greet him when he arrived home from work. Some days my husband would voluntarily do the dishes or wash a load of clothes, without me asking him to do so. In addition, he would cook dinner on the weekends when he had time, and he would enjoy doing it. His actions communicated to me that he knew I was tired, and he wanted to do his share of the housework. To me, this was more romantic than telling me he loved me because he actually showed me how he felt by the service he rendered.

3. Expressing Kindness to Your Spouse

There are times when we all want someone to let us know we are special to them. It does not take a lot of time to pick up a small gift for your spouse. This will be a way to communicate to them that you were thinking about them. It does not have to be a special occasion, such as their birthday or anniversary. You may just happen to see an item you think they may enjoy and decide to purchase it for your husband or wife. There's nothing like being surprised by a lovely gift from your spouse for no particular reason other than, "Just because they love you." This can be an act of kindness that brightens the day for your mate. It may have been a bad day for them at work, and you have done something to lift their spirit.

Men can also show kindness by offering to stay home with the kids while your spouse goes out with a friend or relative, or you may just offer to wash your spouse's car. Likewise, the wife can cook her husband's favorite meal or treat him to a movie he will enjoy. These are all ways to express appreciation to your mate.

4. Celebrating Accomplishments

It is important to share joyous occasions with your spouse and others. It is a way of communicating to your spouse and the world that you are proud of them. For example, when my husband was named Pastor of our church, I mailed invitations to his installation service and hosted a reception for him. This was an accomplishment he had achieved, and I wanted to invite our friends and relatives to come celebrate with us. Afterwards, my husband told me how good he felt that I worked so hard to plan a special celebration for him. This was a way for me to show my husband that I respected and loved him.

5. Speaking Positive Words of Encouragement

It has been my experience that everyone likes to hear positive words spoken to them. There is another cliché which states: "You can attract more flies with honey than you can with vinegar." There is no question that positive words can create positive results.

It's important for spouses to say positive words of affirmation about their spouse. For example, my husband has often said publicly that he is proud of me being his wife, and he respects me for raising our children. He has publicly proclaimed, many times, that I have been a good wife and mother. I have also expressed my love for him by speaking positive words to him.

Recently, when we went to pick out a new car for me, my husband suggested that I get a car with a full navigation system. Although I replied that I could manage driving without a navigation feature, he stated that he was willing to spend more money to make sure I would be safe and not get lost. After we drove the new car home, I told him that I appreciated the way he showed his love and concern for my safety. I said to him, "David, that's one reason I'm glad I married you."

I have also encouraged him in pursuing his goals and objectives in life. A month after he enrolled in a Doctoral program in Ministry, he became discouraged and told me he was not sure if he could finish all of the work. I encouraged him to continue in the program, and I offered to proofread his papers for him. One year later, he is doing very well in completing the program, and he will finish in a few months. This is an example of how positive words of affirmation have been helpful in showing my love and support for my husband.

6. Do Not Shame Your Spouse

You should always avoid shaming your spouse before others. The complete opposite action of saying positive words before others about your spouse is saying negative words. No one, male or female, wants to be shamed or "put down" before other persons.

Just like you can build up your spouse's confidence and self-esteem by saying good things about them, you can just as easily tear down their confidence by saying negative things to them. In the scripture, James chapter 4, the writer speaks against saying negative things about others:

> "Speak not evil one of another, brethren. He that speaketh evil of his brother, and judgeth his brother, speaketh evil of the law, and judgeth the law: but if thou judge the law, thou art not a doer of the law, but a judge." James 4:11.

Similarly, in Ephesians 5:22 KJV, Paul tells wives to respect their husbands by stating: "Wives, submit to your husband as to the Lord." This means that wives should show respect by their actions as well as words. By shaming her husband, a wife is not being respectful to him.

Paul also speaks to husbands in Ephesians 5:25 by saying: "Husbands, love your wives, just as Christ loved the church…" Likewise, a man should show love to his wife by the words he speaks to her. By shaming his wife, a man is not showing his wife love.

7. Settling Disputes with Your Spouse

It has been my experience that even when a person loves their spouse, there will be times that the two of you will have a disagreement about something. This is to be expected because husbands and wives are individuals, and everyone does not see things from the same perspective. Each person created by God has different personalities, as well as life experiences that affect our views and opinions about life.

For example, my husband and I have different personalities. David is very outgoing, gregarious, and entertaining. He loves being around other persons all of the time, and he likes to entertain guests frequently. He prides himself on being a great cook, and he enjoys inviting persons to our home for dinner.

I happen to be more reserved and private. Although I enjoy entertaining guests and inviting friends over for dinner, I do not feel a need to do so for every holiday or special event we celebrate. I am content having dinner with the family and a few friends every now and then.

I have learned to "listen" to my husband and try to see things regarding socializing from his perspective. During the early years of our marriage, our most frequent disagreements were about his desire to always invite his friends and family over just to socialize. It didn't even have to be a holiday or special occasion.

After a few years, I realized that if I objected about him frequently inviting guests to our home, he would not be happy. Also, I realized that he grew up in the South, and his family was very hospitable and friendly to everybody. David had six siblings, and they always enjoyed spending time together, along with his parents, not to mention the other aunts, uncles, and cousins who always came to visit their home.

I made an effort to see things from his perspective and to be more accommodating. I realized that there was nothing wrong with what he wanted to do, and I had to learn to put my feelings aside and go along with his plans. It helped to know he was willing to do most of the cooking, and he would help me in cleaning up afterwards. So instead of the guests being "his company," they became "our company." Also, I realized that when he was happy, he was much easier to live with.

Now there is another cliché which says: "What's good for the goose is also good for the gander." This means that during the years of our marriage, David has learned to go along with my way of thinking sometimes when he did not fully agree, as long as it was not harmful to us or did not "bust our budget." In most cases, even though we may have disagreed initially about doing something one of us wanted to do, we were able to come together and compromise so that both of us were satisfied with the final outcome.

I believe that effective communication is essential to maintain a happy marriage. There have been numerous books written about the importance of communication between husband and wife. One of my favorite books written on this topic is: *The Five Love Languages, How to Express Heartfelt Commitment to Your Mate* by Gary Chapman. Two other books which have very extensive discussions on good communication are: *Strengthening Your Marriage* by Wayne A. Mack and *How to Improve Your Marriage Without Talking About It*, by Patricia Love and Steven Stosny. After over 30 years of marriage, I believe that communication is essential to maintain a good marriage relationship.

Chapter 7 – Communication Is Basic

Review Questions

1. What does Ephesians 4:29 say about how you should speak to others?
   _____
   _____
   _____

2. What are the elements of effective communication between you and your spouse?
   _____
   _____
   _____

3. What is the most common way persons communicate with their spouse?
   _____
   _____
   _____

4. What are seven other ways to communicate effectively with your spouse?
   _____
   _____
   _____

5. What are some new techniques you are willing to try to improve the communications between you and your spouse?
   _____
   _____
   _____

6. What are the names of three other books written about improving communications between husbands and wives?
   _____
   _____
   _____

Chapter 8
Managing Your Finances

"A man's life does not consist in the abundance of his possessions."
Luke 12:15b

Just as a couple must learn to communicate openly about other areas of their relationship; they must come together, as one, in their commitment to one another regarding finances. How a couple manages finances affects the harmony in their marriage. Achieving this harmony will require a willingness to openly discuss and agree on how their money will be managed. We will look at the Biblical basis for finances, financial agreement, and financial responsibility within marriage.

Biblical Principles on Finances

Biblical principles must be adhered to in order to successfully manage your finances. The first responsibility in handling your finances is giving to the Lord.

> "Honor the Lord with your wealth, with the firstfruits of all your crops; then your barns will be filled to overflowing, and your vats will brim over with new wine." Proverbs 3:9-10

The commentary on this passage in the *Life Application Study Bible* clearly demonstrates that the priority of giving to God first is a Biblical principle.[15] Giving to God first will be a bridge over greed and will put you in the place to receive God's blessings. Giving to God should have priority in your budget and in your heart. The following Scriptures clearly demonstrate the value of having a Biblically-based financial plan.

1. Proverb 10:22 – "The blessings of the Lord brings wealth, and add no trouble to it."

2. Genesis 24:35 – "The Lord has blessed my master abundantly, and he has become wealthy. He has given him sheep and cattle, silver and gold, menservants, and maidservants, and camels and donkeys."

3. Deuteronomy 8:18 – "But remember the Lord your God, for it is he who gives you the ability to produce wealth, and so confirms his covenant, which he swore to your forefathers, as it is today."

---

[15] Life Application Study Bible commentary, Proverbs 3:9-10

4. Proverbs 16:16 – "How much better to get wisdom than gold, to choose understanding rather than silver."

5. Malachi 3:8-10 – "Will a man rob God? Yet you rob me. "But you ask, 'How do we rob you?' In tithes and offerings. You are under a curse – the whole nation of you – because you are robbing me. Bring the whole tithe into the store house, that there may be food in my house. Test me in this, says the Lord Almighty."

6. Proverb 22:3 – "A prudent man sees danger and takes refuge, but the simple keep going and suffer for it."

7. Proverb 11:28 – "Whoever trusts in his riches will fall, but the righteous will thrive like a green leaf."

There is a saying, "Don't bite the hand that feeds you." This is an old proverb that has meaning for married couples today. Jesus stated it this way, "For where your treasure is, there your heart will be also." (Luke 12:34) As you and your spouse consider your finances, it is important to make sure that your heart is treasuring the right things to begin with.

Financial Agreement

Agreement on financial matters will come when the two come together with their plan. Both must agree with the financial plan for their family. Both must put away the old ways of handling financial matters and focus on a plan they both can agree with. It is true that with some couples financial conflict comes into play; they don't agree and the family suffers. Conflict can come into play when one spouse thinks money is very important, and the other thinks it is not. One believes the couple must tithe, and the other thinks differently. One would like to eat out several times a week due to his or her heavy work schedule, and the other thinks it is impossible due to a lack of funds. It is essential that the husband and wife openly communicate with each other about their opinion of each other's attitude about spending money and come to an agreement regarding how they will work together to manage their money.

The following example is a story about a couple who did not have a financial agreement. The facts will demonstrate how a family can find themselves in a financial bind because they neglected to manage their finances.

The Smith Family

Janie and Steve Smith just got married. Still enjoying the honeymoon stage of their marriage, they did not focus on their finances. Deeply in love, they both believed that love and sex was enough to sustain them. Janie was a teacher, and Steve worked in the plant as a skilled mechanic.

The first two years of marriage were great. They spent their time at work, and when they returned home, later in the day, they passed their time enjoying each other's undivided attention. In the third year of marriage, they became the proud parents of a baby boy named Bobby. They were both elated about having a healthy son. Janie was allowed six weeks maternity leave from her job. However, she was surprised by the fact she was not nearly ready to return to work at the end of that time. She expressed her desire to stay home longer with the baby, and Steve agreed that he wanted her to take care of their son rather than paying a full-time baby sitter.

After a year passed, Janie still enjoyed being at home, and within another three months she was pregnant again. Janie and Steve discussed the cost of finding a full-time baby sitter as opposed to Janie continuing to stay home. They both agreed that economically, since Steve's salary was enough to pay for the expenses of their home and family, Janie should continue to stay home. Although they seemed to manage paying the bills, Janie was no longer able to spend money on clothing for herself as she did when she worked. Steve began to notice that when he came home, Janie was feeling tired from taking care of Bobby, who was 18 months old and getting into things, all day. In addition, Janie was pregnant and her energy just seemed to disappear after dinner was done. Steve was disappointed often by not having sex with Janie at night because she is tired or just doesn't feel like it.

After their daughter Sally was born, Steve realized that his paycheck had evaporated. What he used to earn just wasn't enough to take care of his wife and two children. Steve rarely spent any romantic time with his wife before she would fall to sleep. To complicate things further, Steve felt neglected at home because Janie was giving all of her attention to the children.

The family budget had doubled in size, but the income has stayed the same. Steve and Janie were forced to deal with their financial situation. They have decided that unless they get their finances under control something will explode, and they hope it won't be their marriage.

How can Steve and Janie begin managing their finances?

First, they must take time to set some financial goals for their family. These should include both long term and short term goals. For example, some long term goals may include saving for a down payment on a house, as well as, investing in a state sponsored fund for their children's college tuition. On the other hand, some short term goals may include increasing their income by Janie returning to work, as well as, becoming current on all of the monthly bills.

Second, they must set a monthly budget which includes their revenues and expenses. Revenues include all monies coming into the household, such as, salaries and money earned by each spouse. Expenses include all monies going out of the household, such as, utilities and telephone bills, food, clothing, car notes and gas, insurance, and monies spent on entertaining. The budget requires both husband and wife to sit down together and list the items included as revenue and expenses. This is the time for couples to agree on which expenses can be modified or even eliminated. This may become an emotional time for spouses because both may have to give up certain things to form a manageable monthly budget. The budget should include a miscellaneous category for unexpected expenses. Of course, a reasonable limit must be set for this. *(See Appendix C – Sample Budget Format.)*

Third, husband and wife must make a commitment to adhere to the monthly budget. Unless both agree to stick with the budget, within reason, their efforts in making the budget will be wasted. Likewise, someone must be responsible for managing the budget. Although, both husband and wife should participate in being responsible for spending money and writing out the bills, one person must take the lead in seeing that the budget is adhered to each month.

In his book entitled, *The Marriage You Always Wanted*, Gary Chapman states:

> "A national survey indicated that 64 percent of American couples frequently quarrel over each other's spending habits and their mutual inability to keep track of money outflow."[16]

He goes on to describe how husbands and wives have different attitudes about managing money. Often, these attitudes are based on strong emotional attachments on how we manage money.

For example, the husband may feel that it is important to have an expensive car, but the wife may feel it is a waste of money. The husband explains that his business image is enhanced by the type of car he drives, and he won't consider driving a less expensive car. On the other hand, the wife feels that a car is just a way to provide transportation, and it should not matter if the car is inexpensive or an older model. Similarly, the wife may have a flair for fashion, and she buys a new outfit every payday. However, her husband is very conservative in buying clothes, and he doesn't agree with his wife's spending habits.

There are so many reasons why couples may disagree, which makes it very important that the couple make an action plan and follow it. This action plan must include a budget upon which both can agree. A realistic assessment of all the household income will make sure that all family needs are included. A detailed list that both spouses agree with should specify how funds are to be disbursed. Clearly this will mean

---

[16] Chapman, 135

determining who is best suited for implementing specific financial responsibilities.

Financial Responsibility

The Bible is clear that the husband is the head of the wife (Ephesians 5:23). Since he is the head of the family, he must *lead* in the planning and the execution of any plans he and his wife agree upon. Being the head of the family clearly places the responsibility for finances on the husband. This does not mean that the wife does not contribute financially or does not assist with disbursing funds; in fact, she may be a homemaker or employed making a salary equal to or greater than the husband. That said, the wise husband will not behave as a dictator regarding how things go, but will include his wife in the decision-making process. While the husband is ultimately responsible before God for his family's well being, both husband and wife are to be financially responsible.

Financial responsibility means living within the level of your earnings and not making debts or obligations which will be difficult to pay out of your actual income. Financial responsibility means choosing not to charge things on your credit card just because you haven't reached your limit. It means living within an agreed upon budget for the household. However, if expenses exceed revenues then maybe trimming extras or obtaining a part-time job will help to balance things. The husband more than likely will have to consider adding something to make revenues equal or exceed expenses. Remember, since the husband is the head, he therefore, must take the lead.

Family finances have changed greatly during the past thirty years in the United States. During this time, more women have entered the workforce as full-time workers. As a result, many wives may earn more money than their husbands. This situation is very common today, particularly since the job market has been quite weak, and many men have lost jobs. Under these circumstances, the husband may not be the primary breadwinner in the family. This raises an interesting question: Does the fact that women may be the primary source of income in the home change the position of the husband being the head of the household?

Recently, a survey of twenty-one married couples was taken. The purpose of the survey was to find out their opinions about managing finances in their home. The results gathered from the survey can be reviewed in Appendix B.

After reviewing the answers, I have observed two important things. First, regarding head of household, most husbands and wives stated that the man/husband is the head according to the Bible. There was no caveat for the amount of financial contribution the husband made to the family. Second, regarding the primary breadwinner, most husbands and wives agreed that the primary breadwinner could be the husband or the wife.

Although men and women may have different opinions about how the money should be managed in their home, the role of the husband is clearly explained in the Bible. Ephesians 5: 23-24 (NKJV) states: "For the husband is head of the wife, as also Christ is head of the church; and He is the Savior of the body. Therefore, just as the church is subject to Christ, so let the wives be to their own husbands in everything." This Scripture states that the husband is the leader in the marriage. I have observed in many marriages that the husband does a very good job in managing the household finances. However,

I have also known several other married couples where the wife takes the lead in managing the finances because she is more skilled in doing so, or because the husband decided not to manage that responsibility.

As we review what we've discussed so far, we understand that maintaining harmony in the marriage regarding finances requires the husband and wife to be willing to:

1. Set financial goals for the family

2. Determine the amount of monthly household revenues

3. Determine the amount of monthly household expenses

4. Make and agree upon a monthly budget

5. Make a commitment to adhere to the budget

Doing these things effectively will mean answering questions such as:

- When bills and other financial debts come into the home, which spouse will gather them?
- How will the spouse know that bills have entered the home?
- Who will actually write the checks?
- Or will the bills be paid online?

While these questions are not a comprehensive list, they will be helpful. Either way, as long as the husband and wife agree on living within their means, and determine who will be responsible for paying the bills, there will be more harmony in their marriage. Regardless of which spouse takes the lead in managing the household finances, he or she should keep the other spouse informed of their current financial status. This will also promote harmony in the marriage.

If you are interested in a more detailed guidance in completing a financial plan, I recommend reading *Your Finances in Changing Times,* by Larry Burkett (1993), pages 131-155. The author lists many questions a married couple needs to answer in preparing a family budget. The information explains the importance of various factors including: personal goals, marriage goals, family goals, financial goals, and specific steps in completing a family financial budget.

Chapter 8 – Finances

Questions for Discussion

1. What is the first obligation in regards to the family's finances?
   _____
   _____
   _____

2. Why is it important to put God first when it comes to finances?
   _____
   _____
   _____

3. Who has the major responsibility in managing the family's finances?
   _____
   _____
   _____

4. Where does the power to gain wealth come from?
   _____
   _____
   _____

5. Why is it necessary to obtain harmony as it relates to the finances?
   _____
   _____
   _____

6. What must each spouse do in order to gain harmony with family finances?

_____
_____
_____

7. What happens if harmony is not obtained?

_____
_____
_____

8. Is it necessary to come together when it comes to family finances?

_____
_____

9. Who should take the lead in the planning and execution of financial plans for the family?

_____
_____
_____

10. Explain what it means to be financially responsible in your marriage.

_____
_____
_____

Reference Books

1. Burkett, L. (1993). *Your Finances In Changing Times.* Chicago, IL: Moody Publishers

2. Chapman, G. (1995). *The Five Love Languages, How To Express Heartfelt Commitment To Your Spouse.* Chicago, IL: Northfield Publishing

3. Chapman, G. (2009). *The Marriage You Always Wanted.* Chicago, IL: Moody Publishers

4. Cloud, H., & Townsend, J. (1999). *Boundaries in Marriage.* Grand Rapids, MI: Zondervan

5. Cutrer, W. & Glahn, S. (2007). *Sexual Intimacy in Marriage.* Grand Rapids, MI: Kregel Publications

6. Eggerichs, E. (2004). *Love & Respect: The Love She Most Desires; The Respect He Desperately Needs.* Nashville, TN: Thomas Nelson, Inc.

7. Heuristic. (n.d.) *Merrimam-Webster's Online Dictionary* (11th. Ed.) Retrieved from http://www.m-w.com/dictionary/heuristic

8. Jeremiah, D. (2010). *What The Bible Says About Love Marriage and Sex.* San Diego, CA: Turning Point.

References

9. Love, P., & Stosny, S. (2008). *How to Improve Your Marriage Without Talking About It.* New York, NY: Three Rivers Press

10. Mack, W.A. (1999). *Strengthening Your Marriage.* Phillipsburg, NJ: Presbyterian & Reformed Publishing

11. Meyer, J. (1997). *Managing Your Emotions, Instead of Your Emotions Managing You.* New York, NY: Warner Faith

12. *Oxford American Large Print Thesaurus.* (2006). New York, NY: Oxford University, Inc.

13. Reisser, T.K. & Reisser, P.C. (2010). *Your Spouse Isn't The Person You Married.* Carol Stream, IL: Tyndale House Publishers, Inc.

14. *The Holy Bible, New International Version. Life Application Study Bible.* (1995). Wheaton, IL: Tyndale House Publishers, Inc.

15. *The International Encyclopedia of Marriage and Family* (2003). New York, NY: Macmillan Reference USA

Appendix A

Chapter 3 – Reflection Questions
"Mutual Support & Respect"

1. I feel comfortable depending on my spouse for support.
   True _____ False _____

2. I do things to support my spouse without being asked.
   True _____ False _____

3. I think my relationship with my spouse can be improved by offering to support him/her more often. **Circle him or her.**
   True _____ False _____

4. I am willing to change my behavior which I know aggravates my spouse.
   True _____ False_____

5. I have spoken with my spouse about changing a behavior which aggravates me.
   True _____ False _____

6. I have seen an improvement in our relationship since requesting the change.
   True _____ False_____

7. Giving mutual support to my spouse is a way of showing respect?
   True _____ False_____

8. Both men and women greatly desire to be loved and respected by their spouse.
   True_____ False _____

9. Men are often attempt to avoid the feeling of "shame."
   True _____ False_____

10. Women are often attempt to avoid the feeling of "fear."
    True _____ False_____

11. Men desire "respect" from their spouse more than love?
    True _____ False_____

12. Women desire "love" and protection from their spouse more than "respect."
    True _____ False_____

13. I am a male.
    True _____ False_____

14. I am a female.
    True _____ False_____

15. How long have you been married to your spouse?
 Please check one.

   ❏ 1 - 5 yrs.

   ❏ 6 – 12 yrs.

   ❏ 13 – 20 yrs.

   ❏ 21 – 30 yrs.

   ❏ 31 – 60 yrs.

Additional comments:
_____
_____
_____
_____
_____
_____
_____

For a printer-friendly version of this questionnaire to use with your group, visit my website.

Appendix A
Chapter 3 – Survey Results
"Mutual Support & Respect"

Number of Surveys Distributed: 26

Number of Surveys Returned: 26
(12 Husbands; 14 Wives)

Number of Years Married: 6 to 51 years

Average Years Married: 23

Appendix A
Chapter 3 – Reflection Responses
"Mutual Support & Respect"

QUESTIONS	T/F	MALE	FEMALE
1. I feel comfortable depending on my spouse for support	T	10	14
	F	2	0
2. I do things to support my spouse without being asked.	T	12	14
	F	0	0
3. I think my relationship w/spouse can be improved by offering to support him/her more often	T	12	12
	F	0	2
4. I am willing to change my behavior which I know aggravates my spouse.	T	11	13
	F	1	1
5. I have spoken w/spouse about changing a behavior which aggravates me.	T	9	13
	F	3	1
6. I have seen an improvement in our relationship since requesting the change.	T	7	8
	F	3	5
	NA	2	1
7. Giving mutual support to my spouse is a way of showing respect.	T	12	14
	F	0	0

Chapter 3 – Reflection Responses Cont'd

QUESTIONS	T/F	MALE	FEMALE
8. Both men and women greatly desire to be loved and respected by their spouse.	T	12	14
	F	0	0
9. Men often attempt to avoid the feeling of shame.	T	10	14
	F	2	0
10. Women often attempt to avoid the feeling of fear.	T	10	10
	F	2	4
11. Men desire respect from their spouse more than love.	T	12	13
	F	0	1
12. Women desire love and protection from spouse more than respect.	T	10	10
	F	2	4

Appendix B

Chapter 8 – Reflection Questions
"Managing Your Finances"

Making Money an Asset and Not an Attack on Marriage

Number Years Married: _____ ❏ Husband ❏ Wife

I am a:
- ❏ Housewife
- ❏ Primary Bread Winner
- ❏ Retired
- ❏ Self-employed
- ❏ Saver
- ❏ Tither
- ❏ House husband
- ❏ Secondary Bread Winner
- ❏ Retired and working part time
- ❏ Unemployed
- ❏ Spender
- ❏ Non-Tither

I have a:
- ❏ Joint Checking Account With Spouse
- ❏ Joint Checking Account With my child (or children)
- ❏ Personal Checking Account
- ❏ Joint Savings Account With Spouse
- ❏ Joint Savings Account With my child (or children)
- ❏ Personal Savings Account

The Head of the Household should always be the Primary Bread Winner.

❏ Yes   ❏ No

Briefly Explain:

_____
_____
_____
_____

Our household finances are managed by:

❑ Husband   ❑ Wife

All that we have, including our finances, belong to:

❑ Husband   ❑ Wife   ❑ Husband & Wife   ❑ God

❑ Other: _____

My spouse and I agree on how finances are managed in our marriage and we are blessed:

❑ Yes   ❑ No   ❑ Working on it!

For a printer-friendly version of this questionnaire to use with your group, visit my website.

Appendix B
Financial Management Survey Results

Number of Surveys Distributed: 26

Number of Surveys Returned: 21
(10 Husbands; 11 Wives)

Number of Years Married: 6 to 51 years

Average Years Married: 23

Harmony in Marriage: More Than Sex

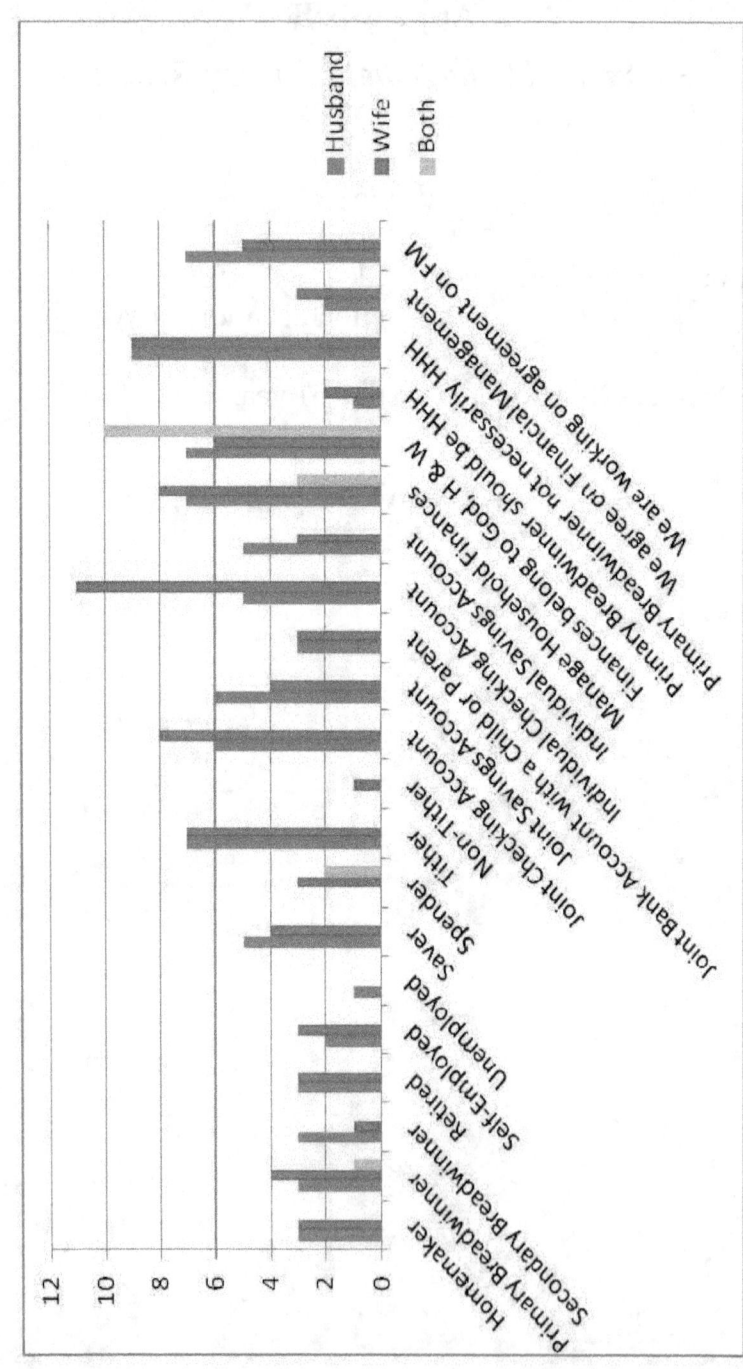

Financial Management Survey Results Chart

Note: Answers do not add up as some participants left certain questions blank, or they endorsed two answers for the same question, i.e., "saver and spender."

Financial Management Survey Results Cont'd

QUESTIONS	Husband	Wife	Both
1. Homemaker	3	3	0
2. Primary Breadwinner	3	4	1
3. Secondary Breadwinner	3	1	0
4. Retired	3	3	0
5. Self-employed	2	3	0
6. Unemployed	1	0	0
7. Saver	5	4	0
8. Spender	0	3	2
9. Tither	7	7	0
10. Non-tither	0	1	0
11. Joint Checking Account	6	8	0
12. Joint Savings Account	6	4	0
13. Joint Bank Account with a Child or Parent	3	3	0
14. Individual Checking Account	5	11	0
15. Individual Savings Account	5	3	0
16. Manage Household Finances	7	8	3
17. Finances belong to God, H & W	7	6	10
18. Primary Breadwinner should be HHH	1	2	0
19. Primary Breadwinner is not necessarily HHH	9	9	0
20. We agree on Financial Management	2	3	0

Appendix C
Chapter 8 – Sample Budget Format
Adapted from Your Finances in Changing Times

GROSS INCOME
PER MONTH _____
Salary _____
Interest _____
Dividends _____
Other _____

LESS:
1. **Tithe** _____
2. **Tax** _____

NET SPENDABLE
INCOME _____

3. **Housing**
   Mortgage _____
   Insurance _____
   Taxes _____
   Electricity _____
   Gas _____
   Water _____
   Sanitation _____
   Telephone _____
   Maintenance _____
   Other _____

4. **Food** _____

5. **Automobile** _____
   Payments _____
   Gas & Oil _____
   Insurance _____
   License/Taxes _____
   Maint/Repair _____

6. **Insurance** _____
   Life _____
   Medical _____
   Other _____

7. **Debts** _____
   Credit Card _____
   Loans & Notes _____
   Other _____

8. **Entertainment**
   & Recreation _____
   Eating Out _____
   Baby Sitters _____
   Activities/Trips _____
   Vacation _____
   Other _____

9. **Clothing** _____

10. **Savings** _____

11. **Medical Expenses** _____
    Doctor _____
    Dentist _____
    Drugs _____
    Other _____

12. **Miscellaneous** _____
    Toiletry, cosmetics _____
    Beauty, barber _____
    Laundry, cleaning _____
    Allowances, lunches _____
    Subscriptions _____
    Gifts (incl. Christmas) _____
    Cash _____
    Other _____

13. **School/Child Care** _____
    Tuition _____
    Materials _____
    Transportation _____
    Day Care _____

14. **Investments** _____

15. **Unallocated Surplus**
    Income * _____

   TOTAL EXPENSES _____

INCOME VS. EXPENSES
   Net Spendable Income _____
   Less Expenses _____

* This category is used when surplus income is received. This would be kept in the checking account to be used within a few weeks; otherwise, it should be transferred to an allocated category.

Burkett, L. (1993).

Biography

Reverend Catherine Roberson was born and grew up in Detroit, MI. She always enjoyed learning and achieving academic goals. Reverend Catherine has a Bachelor of Arts degree from the University of Michigan, Ann Arbor, MI; a Master of Arts Degree in Pastoral Ministry from Marygrove University, Detroit, MI; and a Juris Doctorate Degree from Rutgers University, School of Law, in New Jersey.

Reverend Catherine was licensed at New Hope Missionary Baptist Church, located in Southfield, MI in 2001 and ordained in 2005. She serves as a Pulpit Minister at New Hope MBC and assists her husband, Pastor David L. Roberson. Reverend Catherine also serves as the Minister of the Women of Hope, and in 2006, she founded and directs the Health and Healing Ministry. New Hope MBC has sponsored many annual community health fairs under the leadership of Reverend Catherine. During these community events, hundreds of persons have received free medical tests and educational workshops about health and wellness.

Reverend Catherine has received several awards from public service organizations. In 2005, Delta Sigma Theta Sorority, S.A.C., awarded Reverend Catherine with the Torch Award, for Outstanding Ministry and Community Service. Also, Reverend Catherine was recognized, by the

Board of Directors of the Gospel Against AIDS in 2009, for her work in sponsoring HIV/AIDS testing and awareness workshops at her church.

Reverend Catherine has been happily married to her husband for more than thirty years. They have two adult children, Minister Justice Roberson and Minister Crystal Wilson. Both of their children are college graduates and have successful business careers.

Reverend Catherine Roberson has faced many challenges in her life. She was one of six children raised by a divorced mother. Also, she was the first female in her family to graduate from college and later law school. She has also endured the tests of being married to a Baptist Pastor while having a career in Michigan state government and raising a family. However, she gives the Lord all the credit for making her and her family spiritually strong.

www.ingramcontent.com/pod-product-compliance
Lightning Source LLC
Chambersburg PA
CBHW052102070526
44584CB00017B/2303